A Day in the Life: Rainforest Animals

Anaconda

Anita Ganeri

www.raintreepublishers.co.uk
Visit our website to find out
more information about
Raintree books.

To order:

☎ Phone 0845 6044371

📄 Fax +44 (0) 1865 312263

💻 Email myorders@raintreepublishers.co.uk

Customers from outside the UK please telephone +44 1865 312262

Raintree is an imprint of Capstone Global Library Limited,
a company incorporated in England and Wales having its
registered office at 7 Pilgrim Street, London, EC4V 6LB –
Registered company number: 6695582

Text © Capstone Global Library Limited 2011
First published in hardback in 2011
Paperback edition first published in 2012
The moral rights of the proprietor have been asserted.

Edited by Nancy Dickmann, Rebecca Rissman,
   and Catherine Veitch
Designed by Steve Mead
Picture research by Mica Brancic
Originated by Capstone Global Library
Printed and bound in China by South China Printing
   Company Ltd

ISBN 978 1 4062 1655 4 (hardback)
14 13 12 11 10
10 9 8 7 6 5 4 3 2 1

ISBN 978 1 4062 1875 6 (paperback)
15 14 13 12 11
10 9 8 7 6 5 4 3 2 1

British Library Cataloguing in Publication Data
Ganeri, Anita
Anaconda. -- (A day in the life. Rainforest animals)
597.9'67-dc22
A full catalogue record for this book is available from the
British Library.

Acknowledgements
We would like to thank the following for permission to
reproduce photographs: Ardea **p. 16** (Francois Gohier);
Corbis **p. 17** (© Joe McDonald); Getty Images **p. 22** (Dorling
Kindersley); FLPA **pp. 6** (Minden Pictures/Claus Meyer),
9, **18**, **23 swamp** (Jurgen & Christine Sohns), **13** (Minden
Pictures/Heidi & Hans-Juergen Koch); Photolibrary **pp. 4**
(Animals Animals/Francois Savigny), **5**, **23 reptile** (First Light
Associated Photographers/Philippe Henry), **7**, **23 camouflage**
(age fotostock/Morales Morales), **14**, **23 capybara** (F1 Online/
Ritterbach Ritterbach), **20** (age fotostock/Berndt Fischer), **21**
(Juniors Bildarchiv); Photolibrary [Rex Features] **p. 19** (age
fotostock/Morales Morales); Photoshot/NHPA **pp. 10**, **11**, **12**,
15, **23 jaws**, **23 prey**; Shutterstock **p. 23 rainforest** (© Szefei).

Cover photograph of a green anaconda reproduced with
permission of Photolibrary (Animals Animals/Austin
J Stevens).

Back cover photographs of (left) a yellow anaconda
constricting prey reproduced with permission of Photoshot
(NHPA); and (right) a green anaconda (Eunectes murinus)
reproduced with permission of FLPA (Minden Pictures/Heidi
& Hans-Juergen).

We would like to thank Michael Bright for his invaluable help
in the preparation of this book.

Contents

Some words are in bold, **like this**. You can find them in the glossary on page 23.

An anaconda is a type of snake.

All snakes have long, tube-shaped bodies with a head at one end and a tail at the other.

alligator

Anacondas and other snakes belong to a group of animals called **reptiles**.

Alligators, crocodiles, lizards, turtles, and tortoises are also reptiles.

What does an anaconda look like?

An anaconda has a very long, thick body.

An adult anaconda can grow almost as long as a bus.

An anaconda's skin is dark green or yellow with a pattern of large, black spots.

This helps to **camouflage** the snake.

South America

Anacondas live in the **rainforests** of South America.

It is warm and wet in the rainforest all the year round.

Anacondas like to live in slow-moving streams and **swamps** in the rainforest.

They spend most of their time in the water.

At night, anacondas hunt for food.

They lie in the water and wait for
prey to pass by.

prey

The anaconda grabs its prey in its **jaws**.

It coils, or wraps, its body around the prey and squeezes it to death.

An anaconda can swim very fast to catch its **prey**.

It curves its body from side to side, pushing the water behind it.

nostril

eye

An anaconda's eyes and nostrils are on the top of its head.

This helps it to see and breathe while it is swimming or floating in the water.

capybaras

Anacondas hunt other **rainforest** animals, such as fish, birds, and frogs.

Large anacondas can catch bigger animals, such as **capybaras**.

14

jaws

An anaconda swallows its **prey** whole, head first.

Its **jaws** are held together by stretchy bands so it can open its mouth very wide.

What does an anaconda do after feeding?

food

It takes an anaconda a long time to take in food.

It lies on the riverbank or in the water, hardly moving at all.

After a big meal, an anaconda may not need to eat again for several weeks, or even months.

Then it goes hunting again.

What do young anacondas look like?

baby

Many snakes lay eggs, but anacondas have babies that look like small adults.

A female anaconda has as many as 40 babies at a time.

Baby anacondas are born in the water at night.

Then their mother swims away and leaves them alone.

An anaconda spends the day resting and sleeping.

It cannot close its eyes because it does not have eyelids.

The anaconda's eyes are covered in see-through skin.

This makes its eyes look as if they are staring.

body

tongue

eye

head

tail

skin

camouflage colour or patterns of an animal's fur or skin that help it to hide

capybara rainforest animal that looks like a large guinea pig

jaws top and bottom parts of the mouth

prey animal that is hunted by other animals for food

rainforest thick forest with very tall trees and a lot of rain

reptile animal that has scaly skin, such as a snake or a crocodile

swamp piece of land that is often covered by water

Fi... ...t m..r

Books

Rainforest Animals (Focus on Habitats), Stephen Savage
  (Wayland, 2006)
Usborne Beginners: Rainforest, Lucy Beckett-Bowman
  (Usborne, 2008)

Websites

http://kids.nationalgeographic.com/Animals/CreatureFeature/
  Anaconda
www.unmuseum.org/bigsnake.htm

Index